United States
Indian Policy

BIBLIOGRAPHICAL SERIES

*The Newberry Library Center
for the History of the American Indian*

General Editor
Francis Jennings

The Center Is Supported by Grants from

The National Endowment for the Humanities
The Ford Foundation
The W. Clement and Jessie V. Stone Foundation
The Woods Charitable Fund, Inc.

United States Indian Policy

A Critical Bibliography

FRANCIS PAUL PRUCHA

Published for the Newberry Library

Indiana University Press

BLOOMINGTON AND LONDON

Published in Canada by Fitzhenry & Whiteside Limited, Don Mills,
Ontario

Manufactured in the United States of America

Library of Congress Cataloging in Publication Data
Prucha, Francis Paul.
United States Indian policy.
(Bibliographical series)
Includes index.
1. Indians of North America--Government relations--
Bibliography. I. Title. II. Series.
Z1209.2.U5P673   [E93]   016.3231'19'7073   77-6920
ISBN 0-253-36165-6   1 2 3 4 5 81 80 79 78 77

CONTENTS

THE EDITOR TO THE READER

A massive literature exists for the history and culture of American Indians, but the quality of that literature is very uneven. At its best it compares well with the finest scholarship and most interesting reading to be found anywhere. At its worst it may take the form of malicious fabrication. Sometimes, well-intentioned writers give false impressions of reality either because of their own limitations of mind or because they lack adequate information. The consequence is a kind of chaos through which advanced scholars as well as new students must warily pick their way. It is, after all, a history of hundreds, if not thousands, of human communities spread over an entire continent and enduring through millennia of pre-Columbian years as well as the five centuries that Europeans have documented since 1492. That is not a small amount of history.

Often, however, historians have been so concerned with the affairs of European colonies or the United States that they have almost omitted Indians from their own history. There is a way of writing "frontier history" and the "history of Indian-White relations" that often focuses so narrowly upon the intentions and desires of Euro-Americans as to treat Native Americans as though they were merely natural parts of the landscape, like forests or mountains or wild animals — obstacles to "progress" or "civilization." One of the major purposes of the Newberry Library's Center for the History of the American Indian is to modify that narrow conception; to put Indians properly back into the central role in their own history and into the history of the United States of America as well — as participants in, rather than obstacles to, the creation of American society and culture.

The series of bibliographies of which this book is one part is intended as a guide to reliable sources and studies in particular fields of the general literature. Some of these are devoted to culture areas; others treat selected individual tribes; and a third group speaks to significant contemporary and historical issues.

The present volume is in the last group. It assumes that Indian history of the modern era must be understood in a context that also includes the history of the powerful intervention of non-Indians in Indian affairs.

For example, the reasons that Eastern Indians emigrated beyond the Mississippi included both internal decisions of the tribes and the external pressures imposed upon them by state governments and by the Federal government. Knowledge of the development of the policy of removal is essential for grasping the evolution of such vital modern issues as tribal sovereignty, land tenure, and government. But Indians were not mere physical objects for policy makers to dispose of at will, and the works listed and recommended herein describe active Indian responses and reciprocal effects on policies as well as the intended policies themselves.

This work is designed in a format, standard for the series, intended to be useful to both beginning students and advanced scholars. It has two main parts: the essay (conveniently organized by subheadings) and an alphabetical list of all works cited. All citations in the essay are directly keyed, by means of bracketed numbers, to the more complete publication data in the list; and each item in the list carries a reference to the page number where it is mentioned in the essay. In addition, the series incorporates several information-at-a-glance features. Among them are two sets of recommended titles: a list of five works recommended for the beginner and a group of volumes that constitute a basic library collection in the field. The large, complete list also uses asterisks to denote works suitable for secondary school students. This apparatus has been built in because the bibliographical essay, in a form familiar to scholars, could prove fairly hard going for beginners, who may wish to put it aside until they have gained sufficient background from introductory materials. Such students should come back to the essay eventually, however, because it surveys a vast sweep of information about a great variety of persons, places, communities, and events.

There is variety also in the kinds of sources because these critical bibliographies support the study of ethnohistory. Unlike older, more narrow disciplines, ethnohistory embraces the entire culture of a people; it demands contributions from a wide range of source materials. Not the least of these in the history of American Indians are their own music, crafts, linguistics, and oral traditions. Whenever possible, the authors have included such sources as well as those associated with politics, economics, geography, and so on. It will be recognized that the variety of relevant sources will change with the nature of the topic discussed.

In the last analysis this work, like all other bibliographical devices, is a tool. Each author is an expert who knows the literature and advises what source is most helpful for which purpose, but students must use this help according to their individual purposes and capacities. Many ways suggest themselves. The decision is the reader's own.

INTRODUCTION

Indian groups within the United States are viable communities with their own dynamic forces and their own histories. "Indian history" today is increasingly concerned with the experience of these groups, and tribal patterns of culture and of political organization are becoming better known. These Indian communities, however, did not develop in a social or political vacuum. They interacted with white communities and then, to a large extent, were overcome by the whites — militarily defeated, culturally oppressed, and subjected to a heavy loss of sovereignty and self-determination.

Building on a history of colonial relations with the Indian tribes, the United States government became the primary instrument in this process, for when the new federal nation arose, it was the national government, not the individual states, that became responsible for Indian affairs. As the United States grew in size and power, and as other nations interested in the Indians — specifically Great Britain and Spain — withdrew or were forced out, it was the United States alone with whom the Indian communities within its territorial limits were forced to deal. From the end of the Revolution to the present day the policy of the United States government toward the Indians was a powerful, often decisive element in the history of the Indians. Those who wish to understand Indian history, then, cannot close their eyes to the history of federal Indian policy. And, in fact, there is an almost overwhelming body of records and historical writings to draw on. This, to be sure, is "white history," the history of the dominant American society and its government, written by and large by white historians. But interlaced in the complex story is the history of the Indian groups who were the object of government policies and programs.

An extensive classified listing of books and articles dealing with these matters is Francis Paul Prucha, *A Bibliographical Guide to the History of Indian-White Relations in the United States* [127], which has divisions on general Indian policy and on specific aspects of that policy such as treaties, land, military relations, trade, missions, legal relations, education, and health. The present bibliography is a limited selection from that larger work.

There are a number of recent general studies that trace in some way the course of United States Indian policy. Each one has its own emphasis, of course, but together they offer a solid account of federal policy and of the interaction of the white and Indian societies. A short early work is D'Arcy McNickle, *They Came Here First: The Epic of the American Indian* [94]. The author is a Flathead Indian and writes with special sympathy and understanding of the Indian groups. He later joined with Harold E. Fey to write a similar book, *Indians and Other Americans: Two Ways of Life Meet* [42], and in 1973 he published an excellent account of the ups and downs of tribal existence in contact with white society, *Native American Tribalism: Indian Survivals and Renewals* [93]. Two similarly brief accounts by white scholars are *American Indians* [56], by William T. Hagan, which details white policy toward the Indians, and *A Short History of the In-*

dians of the United States[143], by Edward H. Spicer, in which the author's focus is the history of the Indian communities themselves. Of value also are Angie Debo, *A History of the Indians of the United States* [27], a long book that explicitly emphasizes the Indians of Oklahoma, and S. Lyman Tyler, *A History of Indian Policy* [151], a factual survey written for the Bureau of Indian Affairs with little attempt at critical interpretation. The most recent general account — and in many respects the best — is *The Indian in America* [165], by Wilcomb E. Washburn. Although it is heavily weighted toward colonial beginnings and the early national period, it is a judicious account by a person of deep sympathy for the Indian side of the story.

Recommended Works

For the Beginner

[56]   William T. Hagan, *American Indians.*

[93]   D'Arcy McNickle, *Native American Tribalism: Indian Survivals and Renewals.*

[119]   Kenneth R. Philp, *John Collier's Crusade for Indian Reform, 1920–1954.*

[159]   Dale Van Every, *Disinherited: The Lost Birthright of the American Indian.*

[165]   Wilcomb E. Washburn, *The Indian in America.*

For a Basic Library Collection

[27]   Angie Debo, *A History of the Indians of the United States.*

[56]   William T. Hagan, *American Indians.*

[70]   Reginald Horsman, *Expansion and American Indian Policy, 1783–1812.*

[75]   Alvin M. Josephy, Jr., *Red Power: The American Indians' Fight for Freedom.*

[93]   D'Arcy McNickle, *Native American Tribalism: Indian Survivals and Renewals.*

[119] Kenneth R. Philp, *John Collier's Crusade for Indian Reform, 1920–1954.*

[123] Francis Paul Prucha, *American Indian Policy in Crisis: Christian Reformers and the Indian, 1865–1900.*

[125] Francis Paul Prucha, *American Indian Policy in the Formative Years: The Indian Trade and Intercourse Acts, 1790–1834.*

[136] Ronald N. Satz, *American Indian Policy in the Jacksonian Era.*

[139] Bernard W. Sheehan, *Seeds of Extinction: Jeffersonian Philanthropy and the American Indian.*

[143] Edward H. Spicer, *A Short History of the Indians of the United States.*

[150] Robert A. Trennert, Jr., *Alternative to Extinction: Federal Indian Policy and the Beginnings of the Reservation System, 1846–51.*

[151] S. Lyman Tyler, *A History of Indian Policy.*

[159] Dale Van Every, *Disinherited: The Lost Birthright of the American Indian.*

[165] Wilcomb E. Washburn, *The Indian in America.*

BIBLIOGRAPHICAL ESSAY

Early National Period

Much of the later history was determined in the first decades of the new nation's existence — the treaty system, land cessions, trade regulations, and laws governing intercourse between the two societies. These elements and related affairs have been thoroughly studied. *American Indian Policy in the Formative Years: The Indian Trade and Intercourse Acts, 1790–1834* [125], by Francis Paul Prucha, is a detailed survey of the period to 1834, with a focus on the series of laws which, as supplements to the treaties, determined Indian affairs. It discusses the development of the Indian service, the control of the liquor trade, removal of intruders from Indian lands, punishment of crimes committed in the Indian country, and civilization and removal programs. A similar period is covered by another general work, George Dewey Harmon, *Sixty Years of Indian Affairs, Political, Economic, and Diplomatic, 1789–1850* [63], which is full of details on diplomatic, financial, and educational matters.

Particular aspects of the period are treated in separate studies. The late eighteenth century is covered in Walter H. Mohr, *Federal Indian Relations, 1774–1788* [104], and in Randolph C. Downes, *Council Fires on the Upper Ohio: A Narrative of Indian Affairs in the Upper Ohio Valley until 1795* [36]. Downes deals with relations with the southern tribes in the same period in a series of articles [35, 37, 38, 40]. See also Kenneth Coleman, "Federal Indian Relations in the South, 1781–1789" [22], and the article by R. S. Cotterill, "Federal Indian Management in the South, 1789–1835" [24]. Robert W. McCluggage investigates policy in regard to Indian land titles in the first quarter of the century in a brief article, "The Senate and Indian Land Titles, 1800–1825" [92].

The philosophical basis for Jeffersonian Indian policy is the subject of *Seeds of Extinction: Jeffersonian Philanthropy and the American Indian* [139], by Bernard W. Sheehan. The book traces the benevolent ideas of Jefferson and his contemporaries toward the Indians and the deleterious effects their policies actually had on them. The practical working out of the early policies is described in Reginald Horsman, *Expansion and American Indian Policy, 1783–1812* [70], which sees white avarice for land as the motive force and the humanitarian assertions as justification for it. Horsman has explored other aspects of the problem in his articles, "American Indian Policy in the Old Northwest, 1783–1812" [69], and "American Indian Policy and the Origins of Manifest Destiny" [68].

The federal government's humane concern for the Indians, as well as its rivalry with the British for Indian allegiance and friendship, resulted in the establishment of government trading posts in the Indian country. This "factory system," which ran from 1795 to 1822, can be studied in Ora Books Peake, *A History of the United States Indian Factory System, 1795–1822* [113], and in the following articles: Katherine Coman, "Government Factories:

An Attempt to Control Competition in the Fur Trade"
[23]; Royal B. Way, "The United States Factory System
for Trading with the Indians, 1796–1822" [169]; and
Edgar B. Wesley, "The Government Factory System
among the Indians, 1795–1822" [170]. The development of the Indian service within the War Department
after the War of 1812 was largely the work of the second
superintendent of the factory system, Thomas L.
McKenney, who in 1824 became the first head of the
Indian Bureau. His work and influence are the subject of
the sympathetic scholarly study by Herman J. Viola,
*Thomas L. McKenney: Architect of America's Early Indian
Policy, 1816–1830* [160].

Indian Removal

The 1830s were marked by massive Indian removals,
as the eastern Indians were forced to vacate their homes
east of the Mississippi and accept in exchange new lands
in the West. The policy of removal, first suggested by
President Jefferson in 1803, when the Louisiana Pur-
chase made it feasible, was greatly accelerated in the
1820s. The dynamic westward thrust of the plantation
system in the South threatened the remaining landhold-
ings of the Five Civilized Tribes, and expanding agricultural pioneers in the North pushed out the small and
weak tribal remnants there. Georgia's attack upon the
Cherokees within the state was the most remarkable ac-
tivity, and the removal of the Cherokees has been the
subject of much study. President Andrew Jackson's sup-

port of removal won him the enmity of contemporary Indians and their friends and the criticism of many historians. The arguments pro and con were thoroughly aired at the time, and the historical literature is vast.

The monograph by Annie Heloise Abel, "The History of Events Resulting in Indian Consolidation West of the Mississippi" [4], although old, is still a very useful compendium of data. Reginald Horsman gives valuable background in *The Origin of Indian Removal, 1815–1824* [71], and William Miles has studied the relation of the idea of Negro colonization to the removal of the Indians in " 'Enamoured with Colonization': Isaac McCoy's Plan of Indian Reform" [103]. A well-written, pro-Indian account is Dale Van Every, *Disinherited: The Lost Birthright of the American Indian* [159], and most historians hold similar anti-Jackson positions. A statement more favorable to Jackson than the traditional view is Francis Paul Prucha's article, "Andrew Jackson's Indian Policy: A Reassessment" [126]. An attempt to explain Jackson's support of removal in Freudian terms is made by Michael Paul Rogin in *Fathers and Children: Andrew Jackson and the Subjugation of the American Indian* [134]. The allotment of lands to Indians in the East, as a correlative of removal, is the subject of Mary E. Young's book, *Redskins, Ruffleshirts, and Rednecks: Indian Allotments in Alabama and Mississippi, 1830–1860* [175], and her article, "Indian Removal and Land Allotment: The Civilized Tribes and Jacksonian Justice" [174]. Studies of the removal of particular tribes are Arthur H. DeRosier, Jr., *The Removal of the Choctaw Indians* [33], and Thurman Wilkins, *Cherokee*

Tragedy: The Story of the Ridge Family and the Decimation of a People [172], a special treatment of the protreaty faction of the Cherokees. Grant Foreman describes the actual movement of the Indians to the West in great detail in two books, *Indian Removal: The Emigration of the Five Civilized Tribes of Indians* [43] and *The Last Trek of the Indians* [44], which deals with the northern tribes.

For a valuable study of the Supreme Court cases that arose out of Cherokee removal, see Joseph C. Burke, "The Cherokee Cases: A Study in Law, Politics, and Morality" [17]. An article by Edwin A. Miles, "After John Marshall's Decision: *Worcester* v. *Georgia* and the Nullification Crisis" [102], explains changes in opinion regarding removal when South Carolina threatened nullification. A scholarly survey of the whole Jacksonian period is the recent book by Ronald N. Satz, *American Indian Policy in the Jacksonian Era* [136]. These studies are gradually breaking down the old black-and-white stereotypes and polarization of views by showing the complexity of the issues and the importance of political considerations.

After the completion of the removal process about 1840 and the establishment of what historians have called the "permanent Indian frontier," the government and its missionary allies renewed their efforts at education and civilization for the tribes now settled along the border in the West. These reforming attempts are discussed in Francis Paul Prucha's article, "American Indian Policy in the 1840s: Visions of Reform" [124].

Indians and the Expanding West

The goal of protecting the removed Indians in the West and ameliorating their conditons was soon shattered by the spectacular expansion of the nation to the Pacific. The annexation of Texas in 1845, the settlement of the dispute over the Oregon Country in 1846, and the Mexican War and subsequent Mexican Cession of 1848 caused tremendous new pressures on the lands set aside for eastern Indians in the West and new contacts with Indian tribes which had hitherto been outside the orbit of the federal government. Concern for the Indians in Texas, the Pacific Northwest, California, and the new Southwest as well as in the plains and mountains joining the settled states to the newly acquired regions enlarged federal responsibility for Indian affairs. This transition period has been studied by a number of historians. An early work that deals with the breaking up of the permanent Indian frontier established along the western borders of Arkansas and Missouri is James C. Malin, *Indian Policy and Westward Expansion* [97]. The new regions are the subject of Alban W. Hoopes, *Indian Affairs and Their Administration, with Special Reference to the Far West, 1849–1860* [67]. Separate studies have been made of the new territories, among them the following: George Dewey Harmon, "The United States Indian Policy in Texas, 1845–1860" [64]; Lena Clara Koch, "The Federal Indian Policy in Texas, 1845–1860" [84]; William H. Ellison, "The Federal Indian Policy in California,

1846–1860" [41]; Dale L. Morgan, "The Administration of Indian Affairs in Utah, 1851–1858" [105]; and two articles by C. F. Coan, "The First Stage of the Federal Indian Policy in the Pacific Northwest, 1849–1852" [20], and "The Adoption of the Reservation Policy in the Pacific Northwest, 1853–1855" [19]. A thorough treatment of federal policy in the Southwest is Edward Everett Dale, *The Indians of the Southwest: A Century of Development under the United States* [25].

The period after the Mexican War saw the steady formulation of reservation policy as an answer to the problem of protecting the Indians in the face of aggressive white encroachment. This facet of federal Indian policy is discussed in Robert A. Trennert, Jr., *Alternative to Extinction: Federal Indian Policy and the Beginnings of the Reservation System, 1846–51* [150].

Civil War

The Civil War did not stop or even much slow down white expansion in the West and the resultant conflicts with Indians, and it brought additional problems in the management of Indian affairs. One of these was the attachment of the Five Civilized Tribes of Indian Territory to the Confederacy. A full treatment of these Indians is in Annie Heloise Abel's three-volume study *The Slaveholding Indians* [1, 2, 3]. See also her brief summary article, "The Indians in the Civil War" [5]. The relations of the Indians with the Confederacy are treated by Ohland Morton in "Confederate Government Relations with the

Five Civilized Tribes" [106] and by Kenny A. Franks in "The Confederate States and the Five Civilized Tribes: A Breakdown of Relations" [45].

A more general study of Civil War Indian problems is Edmund J. Danziger, Jr., *Indians and Bureaucrats: Administering the Reservation Policy during the Civil War* [26], which discusses both the events of the period and the effect they had on the administrative functioning of the Indian Bureau. Harry Kelsey writes about Lincoln's Commissioner of Indian Affairs in "William P. Dole and Mr. Lincoln's Indian Policy" [82].

Post–Civil War Indian Reform

Indian affairs were in a state of crisis at the close of the Civil War. The drive of white population both from the east in the traditional movement of agricultural pioneers and from the west as the mining frontier spread into the mountain areas from California caught the Indians in a closing vise. The resistance to these encroachments and to the railroads that speeded them up caused Indian wars of increasing violence. Although the Indian wars that defeated the Indians and forced them to live on reservations were dramatic and are well known, concurrent attempts to reform Indian affairs and replace war by peace are equally significant. These post–Civil War reform movements, sparked by Christian humanitarians, have been studied at some length. There are four general works that survey all or part of the movement to reform Indian policy after 1865. The oldest is Loring B. Priest, *Uncle Sam's Stepchildren: The Reformation of United States Indian Policy, 1865–1887* [122], which traces the failure of the initial reforms under President Grant's "peace policy" and sees the effective culmination of the reform impulse in the Dawes Act (General Allotment Act) of 1887. A second book, covering a similar period, is Henry E. Fritz, *The Movement for Indian Assimilation, 1860–1890* [48], which focuses chiefly on the peace policy under Grant. Robert Winston Mardock, in *The Reformers and the American Indian* [98], is interested primarily in the immediate post–Civil War reformers, who he asserts were a carryover from antislavery reform; but his final chapters deal with the second stage of reform that began about 1880. A broader survey of the period is Francis Paul Prucha, *American Indian Policy in Crisis: Christian Reformers and the Indian, 1865–1900* [123]. This book traces the whole period from 1865 to 1900, but its focus is on the reform undertaken in the last two decades of the century, when the Board of Indian Commissioners, the Indian Rights Association, and the Lake Mohonk Conference — among other groups — persuaded the government to adopt an Indian policy embodying three basic measures: the allotment of reservation lands to individual Indians; extension of American law and citizenship to the Indians; and a comprehensive government school system for the Indians.

Particular aspects of these reforms are found in special studies. The report of the Joint Committee under Senator James R. Doolittle, which was one of the sparks that ignited the reform movement, is analyzed in "The Doolittle Report of 1867: Its Preparation and Short-comings" [81], by Harry Kelsey. The peace policy of President Grant's administration has received much attention; valuable articles are the following: Henry E. Fritz, "The Making of Grant's Peace Policy" [47]; Robert M. Utley, "The Celebrated Peace Policy of General Grant" [154]; and Henry G. Waltmann, "Circumstantial Reformer: President Grant and the Indian Problem" [162]. The participation of particular denominations in the peace policy is covered by Peter James Rahill in *The Catholic Indian Missions and Grant's Peace Policy, 1870– 1884* [132], and by Robert L. Whitner in "The Methodist Episcopal Church and Grant's Peace Policy: A Study of the Methodist Agencies, 1870–1882" [171]. The dis-sertation by Robert H. Keller, Jr., "The Protestant Churches and Grant's Peace Policy: A Study in Church-State Relations, 1869–1881" [77], is a broad, critical work.

The policy of individualizing Indian land tenure by allotment of lands in severalty was long a basic principle of the reformers, as William T. Hagan points out in his "Private Property: The Indian's Door to Civilization" [59]. The early attempts at allotment are discussed in Paul W. Gates, "Indian Allotments Preceding the Dawes Act" [53], while the Dawes Act itself is the subject of a small book by Wilcomb E. Washburn that combines narrative and a selection of documents, *The Assault on Indian Tribalism: The General Allotment Law (Dawes Act) of 1887* [164], and of D. S. Otis, *The Dawes Act and the Allot-*

ment of Indian Lands [111], which carries the story to 1900. Citizenship for the Indians, another fundamental policy of the reformers, is covered in three articles: Michael T. Smith, "The History of Indian Citizenship" [140]; R. Alton Lee, "Indian Citizenship and the Fourteenth Amendment" [87]; and Gary C. Stein, "The Indian Citizenship Act of 1924" [144]. The question of transferring the Bureau of Indian Affairs to the War Department, which was heatedly discussed for more than a decade after the Civil War, is addressed in articles by Donald J. D'Elia, "The Argument over Civilian or Military Indian Control, 1865–1880" [30], and by Marvin H. Garfield, "The Indian Question in Congress and in Kansas" [52]. Reform organizations have been studied by Henry E. Fritz in "The Board of Indian Commissioners and Ethnocentric Reform, 1878–1893" [46] and by Larry E. Burgess in " 'We'll Discuss It at Mohonk' " [16], a brief history of the Lake Mohonk Conference of Friends of the Indian. Writings by the reformers have been assembled in Francis Paul Prucha, ed., *Americanizing the American Indians: Writings by the "Friends of the Indian" 1880–1900* [130]. Helen Hunt Jackson, who was a kind of one-person reform movement with her indictment of federal Indian policy in *A Century of Dishonor: A Sketch of the United States Government's Dealings with Some of the Indian Tribes* [73], has been critically studied by Ruth Odell in a full biography [109] and by Allan Nevins in a brief article, "Helen Hunt Jackson, Sentimentalist vs. Realist" [108].

Post–Civil War reservations have been assessed in

two articles by William T. Hagan, "Indian Policy after the Civil War: The Reservation Experience" [58] and "The Reservation Policy: Too Little and Too Late" [60]. See also Everett W. Sterling, "The Indian Reservation System on the North Central Plains" [145], and Clark Wissler's descriptions of various aspects of reservation life in *Indian Cavalcade; or, Life on the Old-Time Indian Reservations* [173]. One important element of reservation life, the maintenance of law and order, is treated in detail by William T. Hagan in *Indian Police and Judges: Experiments in Acculturation and Control* [57]. For a consideration of policy directed toward a particular area, see Frank D. Reeve, "The Federal Indian Policy in New Mexico, 1858–1880" [133]. Studies of individual tribes, also, give essential information about reservation life and reservation policy.

Special problems attended Indian policy in the Indian Territory. There the Five Civilized Tribes continued their national existence in spite of the intention of the federal government after the Civil War to move them toward regular territorial status and eventual statehood, a move strongly resisted by the leaders of the Indian nations. Allen G. Applen describes an abortive attempt in this direction in "An Attempted Indian State Government: The Okmulgee Constitution in Indian Territory, 1870–1876" [7], and the story of the political changes that ultimately resulted in the State of Oklahoma is set forth in Roy Gittinger, *The Formation of the State of Oklahoma (1803–1906)* [55]. The Cherokee Commission and the Dawes Commission, which brought allotment and the disintegration of the Indian governments, are covered in articles by Berlin B. Chapman [18] and Loren Nunn Brown [15]. Oklahoma Indian affairs are emphasized in the general history by Angie Debo [27].

The reform impulse, which sought to turn the Indians into patriotic American citizens by destroying tribalism and Indian culture and replacing them with white ways, carried well into the twentieth century, but few historians have turned to this later phase of the Christian-motivated reform. The effect of the acculturation process, however, can be seen in a select group of Indians who organized the Society of American Indians. They are studied in Hazel W. Hertzberg, *The Search for an American Indian Identity: Modern Pan-Indian Movements* [65]. Problems of the period, seen from the viewpoint of President Theodore Roosevelt's Commissioner of Indian Affairs, are reviewed in Francis E. Leupp, *The Indian and His Problem* [88].

Reversal of Policy: The Indian New Deal

A new kind of Indian reform movement developed in the 1920s. Rejecting the philosophy embodied in the reforms of the 1880s and 1890s (of which the Dawes Act was a central feature), new agitators for Indian rights demanded that the Indians be allowed to keep their old ways or return to them if they wished. The individual allotment of land, instead of transforming the Indians into hard-working yeomen, had led to the transfer of Indian lands into the hands of whites, and educational and health programs had largely been failures. The rising reform movement of the 1920s, led by the social reformer John Collier, is well documented in Randolph C. Downes, "A Crusade for Indian Reform, 1922–1934" [39], and is also treated in Margaret G. Szasz, "Indian Reform in a Decade of Prosperity" [147], while special aspects of the movement are described in articles by Kenneth R. Philp, "Albert B. Fall and the Protest from the Pueblos, 1921–23" [114] and "John Collier and the Crusade to Protect Indian Religious Freedom, 1920–1926" [118]. A government-sponsored study of Indian conditions at the end of the decade led to the famous Meriam Report [100], which became a kind of blueprint for further reform.

Changes begun by Herbert Hoover's administration are studied in Kenneth R. Philp, "Herbert Hoover's New Era: A False Dawn for the American Indian, 1929–1932" [115]. The reforms, however, were not accomplished until the New Deal of President Franklin Delano Roosevelt, who appointed John Collier Commissioner of Indian Affairs. In his long tenure, 1933–45, Collier instituted an "Indian New Deal," embodied in the Wheeler-Howard Act (Indian Reorganization Act) of 1934. The new policy repealed the allotment policy and sought to reconstitute communal organization and activities among the Indian tribes. Collier's part in this is described in Kenneth R. Philp's book, *John Collier's Crusade for Indian Reform, 1920–1954* [119], and summarized in an article by the same author, "John Collier and the American Indian, 1920–1945" [116]. Early evaluations of the

Wheeler-Howard Act appear in William H. Kelly, ed., *Indian Affairs and the Indian Reorganization Act: The Twenty Year Record* [80], and in Scudder Mekeel's "An Appraisal of the Indian Reorganization Act" [99]. More recent articles on the Indian New Deal are the following: Henry F. Dobyns, "Therapeutic Experience of Responsible Democracy" [34]; Lawrence C. Kelly, "John Collier and the Indian New Deal: An Assessment" [78]; Kenneth R. Philp, "John Collier and the Controversy over the Wheeler-Howard Bill" [117]; Michael T. Smith, "The Wheeler-Howard Act of 1934: The Indian New Deal" [141]; and Graham D. Taylor, "Anthropologists, Reformers, and the Indian New Deal" [148], and idem, "The Tribal Alternative to Bureaucracy: The Indian's New Deal, 1933–1945" [149]. The second half of S. Lyman Tyler's *A History of Indian Policy* [151] indicates the problems Collier had with his program. A careful study of one tribe, Donald L. Parman's *The Navajos and the New Deal* [112], shows the opposition of this Indian group to Collier and his reforms.

Recent History

The general history of post–New Deal Indian policy can be found in such surveys as those of Angie Debo [27], D'Arcy McNickle [93], and Wilcomb Washburn [165], but the period is still too recent to have produced definitive historical studies. Some aspects, however, have received attention. One of these is the Indian Claims

Commission, a special board established in 1946 to rectify past injustices in the government's dealings with the Indians by determining and paying claims brought against the United States by tribes. Since the commission is still functioning, there has been no final assessment of its work, but a good many articles about it have been published. Useful studies, although now somewhat out of date, are Thomas LeDuc, "The Work of the Indian Claims Commission under the Act of 1946" [86], Nancy Oestreich Lurie, "The Indian Claims Commission Act" [90]; and John T. Vance, "The Congressional Mandate and the Indian Claims Commission" [158].

The 1950s witnessed the beginning of a large migration of Indians from reservations to the cities, spurred to a considerable degree by the relocation program of the federal government. The phenomenon of urban Indians promises to be a lasting one, but federal policy in regard to off-reservation Indians has been slow in being formulated. Among many studies dealing with urbanization, the following can serve as an introduction: La Verne Madigan, *The American Indian Relocation Program* [96]; Elaine M. Neils, *Reservation to City: Indian Migration and Federal Relocation* [107]; and the series of articles in Jack O. Waddell and O. Michael Watson, eds., *The American Indian in Urban Society* [161]. S. Lyman Tyler, in "The Recent Urbanization of the American Indian" [152], gives a general overview.

The Collier program of cultivating Indian community life suffered a severe setback in 1953, when Congress adopted a policy of ending federal responsibility for Indian tribes. This "termination" policy was applied to the Menominee Indians in Wisconsin, the Klamath Indians in Oregon, and several smaller groups. The outcry against the policy was vehement, for the change threatened loss of identity for Indian communities as well as loss of federal services, and the government soon abandoned termination without Indian concurrence. Senator Arthur V. Watkins, one of the sponsors of the program, explained his position in "Termination of Federal Supervision: The Removal of Restrictions over Indian Property and Person" [168], and Oliver La Farge described the process in "Termination of Federal Supervision: Disintegration and the American Indian" [85]. Termination of specific tribes is discussed by Nancy Oestreich Lurie in "Menominee Termination: From Reservation to Colony" [91] and by Susan Hood in "Termination of the Klamath Tribe in Oregon" [66].

The cry of the Indians against termination coincided with a rising movement for self-determination, and federal Indian policy has been influenced by demands for "Red Power." The demands have been clearly set forth in Alvin M. Josephy, Jr., *Red Power: The American Indians' Fight for Freedom* [75], in the statement of Vine Deloria, Jr., in his book, *Behind the Trail of Broken Treaties: An Indian Declaration of Independence* [31], and in the call for return of lands in *One Hundred Million Acres* [83], by Kirke Kickingbird and Karen Ducheneaux. The government's response to the demands, however, is still incomplete.

In recent years government task forces and private commissions have studied the conditions of the Indians. One of the most extensive reports is that of the Commission on the Rights, Liberties, and Responsibilities of the American Indian, prepared by William A. Brophy and Sophie D. Aberle and published in 1966 under the title, *The Indian: America's Unfinished Business* [13]. The study of Alan L. Sorkin, *American Indians and Federal Aid* [142], describes and evaluates federal assistance programs and in doing so presents a valuable picture of Indian conditions.

Special Topics

The policy of the United States toward the Indian had many facets, some of which deserve full bibliographies of their own. One of these is education, the provision of schools for the Indians, which began early in the nineteenth century through encouragement of missionary endeavors and then developed into a massive government school system. A general view is provided in a brief book by Evelyn C. Adams, *American Indian Education: Government Schools and Economic Progress* [6], and Margaret Szasz gives a detailed account of recent educational programs in her book, *Education and the American Indian: The Road to Self-Determination, 1928–1973* [146]. Estelle Fuchs and Robert J. Havighurst, in *To Live on This Earth: American Indian Education* [49], and the report of the Senate's Special Sub-Committee on Indian Education, called *Indian Education: A National Tragedy—A*

National Challenge [72], present a view of present-day conditions.

The legal status of the Indians within American society, a topic that is interwoven into most accounts of Indian policy, is treated specifically by Wilcomb E. Washburn in *Red Man's Land/White Man's Law: A Study of the Past and Present Status of the American Indian* [166]. A massive textbook, *Law and the American Indian: Readings, Notes and Cases* [121], by Monroe E. Price, is full of data but difficult to use. A basic reference work, which is a useful guide to all aspects of the government's dealings with the Indians, is the classic volume by Felix S. Cohen, *Handbook of Federal Indian Law, with Reference Tables and Index* [21].

Christian missionary work with the Indians, although an independent religious and philanthropic enterprise, was closely tied to government policy throughout the nineteenth century, for the Indian Office depended upon the missionaries as agents in the programs for educating and civilizing the Indians. The work of the missionaries is analyzed by Robert F. Berkhofer, Jr., in *Salvation and the Savage: An Analysis of Protestant Missions and American Indian Response, 1787–1862* [10]. R. Pierce Beaver has surveyed missionary-government relations in a book, *Church, State, and the American Indians: Two and a Half Centuries of Partnership in Missions between Protestant Churches and Government* [9], and in an article, "American Missionary Efforts to Influence Government Indian Policy" [8].

The organization and functions of the Bureau of

Indian Affairs have been studied in an older work by Laurence F. Schmeckebier, *The Office of Indian Affairs: Its History, Activities, and Organization* [137]. The activities of agents and superintendents have also received attention; examples are the works of Merritt B. Pound on the Creek agent, *Benjamin Hawkins—Indian Agent* [120]; John L. Loos on the superintendent at St. Louis, "William Clark, Indian Agent" [89]; and two studies about Lewis Cass, long-time superintendent of Indian affairs in Michigan Territory, Elizabeth Gaspar Brown's "Lewis Cass and the American Indian" [14] and Francis Paul Prucha's *Lewis Cass and American Indian Policy* [128]. General works on agents are two articles by Ruth A. Gallaher, "The Indian Agent in the United States before 1850" [50] and "The Indian Agent in the United States since 1850" [51], and Flora Warren Symour, *Indian Agents of the Old Frontier* [138]. William E. Unrau has investigated the role of the agents in "The Civilian as Indian Agent: Villain or Victim?" [153].

Much of United States Indian policy was related to the military encounters with the Indians and the ultimate subjugation of the tribes. There is a vast literature on the Indian wars, but a solid introduction can be obtained from three volumes that survey the whole subject in scholarly fashion: Francis Paul Prucha, *The Sword of the Republic: The United States Army on the Frontier, 1783–1846* [129], and two volumes by Robert M. Utley, *Frontiersmen in Blue: The United States Army and the Indian, 1848–1865* [156] and *Frontier Regulars: The United States Army and the Indian, 1866–1891* [155].

Histories of Tribes

A full understanding of how Indian policy operated can be obtained only by studying individual tribes in their relations with the federal government. It is beyond the scope of this bibliography to list all such tribal histories, but a number are especially worth mentioning for what they tell us about Indian policy: Donald J. Berthrong, *The Southern Cheyennes* [12] and *The Cheyenne and Arapaho Ordeal: Reservation and Agency Life* [11]; Angie Debo's history of the Creeks, *The Road to Disappearance* [29], and her *The Rise and Fall of the Choctaw Republic* [28]; Arrell M. Gibson, *The Chickasaws* [54]; William T. Hagan's history of the Sacs and Foxes [61] and his *United States–Comanche Relations: The Reservation Years* [62]; Alvin M. Josephy, Jr., *The Nez Perce Indians and the Opening of the Northwest* [74]; Lawrence C. Kelly, *The Navajo Indians and Federal Indian Policy, 1900–1935* [79]; the history of the Seminoles by Edwin C. McReynolds [95]; Roy W. Meyer, *History of the Santee Sioux: United States Indian Policy on Trial* [101]; James C. Olson, *Red Cloud and the Sioux Problem* [110]; Robert M. Utley, *The Last Days of the Sioux Nation* [157]; and Morris L. Wardell, *Political History of the Cherokee Nation, 1838–1907* [163].

Documents

For a full history of United States policy, of course, one must study the great bulk of government documents, both those published and those in manuscript form in the National Archives. Small parts of this great mass of material have been published in books of collected documents. The most extensive is Wilcomb E. Washburn's four-volume *The American Indian and the United States: A Documentary History* [167], which includes selections from the annual reports of the Commissioner of Indian Affairs, Congressional debates on Indian matters, laws and ordinances, treaties, and judicial decisions. Unfortunately, there is a good deal of editorializing in the headnotes, which detracts from the documentary nature of the collection. A much smaller collection, although broader in the types of materials selected, is Francis Paul Prucha, ed., *Documents of United States Indian Policy* 131]. Vine Deloria, Jr., in *Of Utmost Good Faith* [32], offers a collection of documents described on the dust jacket as "The Case of the American Indian against the Federal Government of the United States — as documented in treaties, speeches, judicial rulings, congressional bills and hearings from 1830 to the present."

Two works are of special importance in studying federal Indian affairs. One is Charles J. Kappler's compilation of Indian laws and treaties, called *Indian Affairs: Laws and Treaties* [76]. Volume 2 of the five-volume work prints all the official Indian treaties. The other is Charles C. Royce's classic study, *Indian Land Cessions in the United States* [135]. Royce summarized the cession provisions of all the treaties in chronological order and provides a remarkable series of state and territorial maps on which the cessions are plotted out.

Alphabetical List and Index

*Denotes items suitable for secondary school students.

Item no.		Essay page no.
[1]	Abel, Annie Heloise. *The American Indian as Slaveholder and Secessionist: An Omitted Chapter in the Diplomatic History of the Southern Confederacy.* Volume 1 of *The Slaveholding Indians.* Cleveland: Arthur H. Clark Company, 1915.	(12)
[2]	———. *The American Indian as Participant in the Civil War.* Volume 2 of *The Slaveholding Indians.* Cleveland: Arthur H. Clark Company, 1919.	(12)
[3]	———. *The American Indian under Reconstruction.* Volume 3 of *The Slaveholding Indians.* Cleveland: Arthur H. Clark Company, 1925.	(12)
[4]	"The History of Events Resulting in Indian Consolidation West of the Mississippi." *Annual Report of the American Historical Association for the Year 1906,* 1:233–450.	(9)
[5]	———. "The Indians in the Civil War." *American Historical Review* 15 (January 1910): 281–296.	(12)

[6]   Adams, Evelyn C. *American Indian Education: Government Schools and Economic Progress.* New York: King's Crown Press, 1946.   (23)

[7]   Applen, Allen G. "An Attempted Indian State Government: The Okmulgee Constitution in Indian Territory, 1870–1876." *Kansas Quarterly* 3 (Fall 1971): 89–99.   (17)

[8]   Beaver, R. Pierce. "American Missionary Efforts to Influence Government Indian Policy." *Journal of Church and State* 5 (May 1963): 77–94.   (24)

[9]   ———. *Church, State, and the American Indians: Two and a Half Centuries of Partnership in Missions between Protestant Churches and Government.* St. Louis: Concordia Publishing House, 1966.   (24)

[10]   Berkhofer, Robert F., Jr. *Salvation and the Savage: An Analysis of Protestant Missions and American Indian Response, 1787–1862.* Lexington: University of Kentucky Press, 1965. Paperback edition with new introduction, New York: Atheneum, 1972.   (24)

[11]   Berthrong, Donald J. *The Cheyenne and Arapaho Ordeal: Reservation and Agency*

Life. Norman: University of Oklahoma
Press, 1976.   (26)

[12]   _____. *The Southern Cheyennes.* Norman: University of Oklahoma Press,
1963.   (26)

[13]   Brophy, William A., and Sophie D.
Aberle. *The Indian: America's Unfinished
Business.* Report of the Commission on
the Rights, Liberties, and Responsibili-
ties of the American Indian. Norman:
University of Oklahoma Press, 1966.   (23)

[14]   Brown, Elizabeth Gaspar. "Lewis Cass
and the American Indian." *Michigan History* 37 (September 1953): 286–298.   (25)

[15]   Brown, Loren Nunn. "The Dawes
Commission." *Chronicles of Oklahoma* 9
(March 1931): 70–105.   (18)

[16]   Burgess, Larry E. " 'We'll Discuss It at
Mohonk.' " *Quaker History: Bulletin of
Friends Historical Association* 40 (Spring
1971): 14–28.   (16)

[17]   Burke, Joseph C. "The Cherokee Cases:
A Study in Law, Politics, and Morality."
Stanford Law Review 21 (February 1969):
500–531.   (10)

[18]   Chapman, Berlin B. "The Cherokee
Commission, 1889–1893." *Indian Magazine of History* 42 (June 1946): 177–190. (18)

[19]   Coan, C. F. "The Adoption of the Reservation Policy in the Pacific Northwest, 1853–1855." *Oregon Historical Society Quarterly* 23 (March 1922): 1–38.   (12)

[20]   ———. "The First Stage of the Federal Indian Policy in the Pacific Northwest, 1849–1852." *Oregon Historical Society Quarterly* 22 (March 1921): 46–89.   (12)

[21]   Cohen, Felix S. *Handbook of Federal Indian Law, with Reference Tables and Index.* Washington, D.C.: Government Printing Office, 1942. Reprinted, Albuquerque: University of New Mexico Press, 1972.   (24)

[22]   Coleman, Kenneth. "Federal Indian Relations in the South, 1781–1789." *Chronicles of Oklahoma* 35 (Winter 1957–1958): 435–458.   (7)

[23]   Coman, Katherine. "Government Factories: An Attempt to Control Competition in the Fur Trade." *Bulletin of the American Economic Association,* 4th series, no. 2 (April 1911): 368–388.   (8)

[24]   Cotterill, R. S. "Federal Indian Management in the South, 1789–1825." *Mississippi Valley Historical Review* 20 (December 1933): 333–352   (7)

[25]   Dale, Edward Everett. *The Indians of the*

Southwest: A Century of Development under the United States. Norman: University of Oklahoma Press, 1949.   (12)

[26]   Danziger, Edmund J., Jr. *Indians and Bureaucrats: Administering the Reservation Policy during the Civil War.* Urbana: University of Illinois Press, 1974.   (13)

*[27]   Debo, Angie. *A History of the Indians of the United States.* Norman: University of Oklahoma Press, 1970.   (3, 18)

[28]   _____. *The Rise and Fall of the Choctaw Republic.* Norman: University of Oklahoma Press, 1934.   (26)

[29]   _____. *The Road to Disappearance.* Norman: University of Oklahoma Press, 1941.   (26)

[30]   D'Elia, Donald J. "The Argument over Civilian or Military Indian Control, 1865–1880." *Historian* 24 (February 1962): 207–225.   (16)

*[31]   Deloria, Vine, Jr. *Behind the Trail of Broken Treaties: An Indian Declaration of Independence.* New York: Delacorte Press, 1974.   (22)

[32]   Deloria, Vine, Jr., ed. *Of Utmost Good Faith.* San Francisco: Straight Arrow Books, 1971.   (27)

[33]   DeRosier, Arthur H., Jr. *The Removal of the Choctaw Indians.* Knoxville: University of Tennessee Press, 1970.   (9)

[34]   Dobyns, Henry F. "Therapeutic Experience of Responsible Democracy." In *The American Indian Today,* edited by Stuart Levine and Nancy Oestreich Lurie, pp. 171–185. Deland, Florida: Everett/Edwards, 1968.   (20)

[35]   Downes, Randolph C. "Cherokee–American Relations in the Upper Tennessee Valley, 1776–1791." *East Tennessee Historical Society's Publications* 8 (1936): 35–53.   (7)

[36]   _____. *Council Fires on the Upper Ohio: A Narrative of Indian Affairs in the Upper Ohio Valley until 1795.* Pittsburgh: University of Pittsburgh Press, 1940.   (6)

[37]   _____. "Creek–American Relations, 1782–1790." *Georgia Historical Quarterly* 21 (June 1937): 142–184.   (7)

[38]   _____. "Creek–American Relations, 1790–1795." *Journal of Southern History* 8 (August 1942): 350–373.   (7)

[39]   _____. "A Crusade for Indian Reform, 1922–1934." *Mississippi Valley Historical Review* 32 (December 1945): 331–354.   (19)

[40]   _____. "Indian Affairs in the Southwest
          Territory, 1790–1796." *Tennessee His-
          torical Magazine,* 2d series, 3 (January
          1937): 240–268.   (7)

[41]   Ellison, William H. "The Federal Indian
          Policy in California, 1846–1860." *Missis-
          sippi Valley Historical Review* 9 (June
          1922): 37–67.   (12)

*[42]   Fey, Harold E., and D'Arcy McNickle.
          *Indians and Other Americans: Two Ways of
          Life Meet.* New York: Harper and Broth-
          ers, 1959.   (2)

[43]   Foreman, Grant. *Indian Removal: The
          Emigration of the Five Civilized Tribes of
          Indians.* Norman: University of Okla-
          homa Press, 1932.   (10)

[44]   _____. *The Last Trek of the Indians.* Chi-
          cago: University of Chicago Press, 1946.   (10)

[45]   Franks, Kenny A. "The Confederate
          States and the Five Civilized Tribes: A
          Breakdown of Relations." *Journal of the
          West* 12 (July 1973): 439–454.   (13)

[46]   Fritz, Henry E. "The Board of Indian
          Commissioners and Ethnocentric Re-
          form, 1878–1893." In *Indian–White Re-
          lations: A Persistent Paradox,* edited by
          Jane F. Smith and Robert M. Kvasnicka,

pp. 57–78. Washington, D.C.: Howard University Press, 1976. (16)

[47] ——. "The Making of Grant's Peace Policy." *Chronicles of Oklahoma* 37 (Winter 1959–1960): 411–432. (15)

[48] ——. *The Movement for Indian Assimilation, 1860–1890.* Philadelphia: University of Pennsylvania Press, 1963. (14)

[49] Fuchs, Estelle, and Robert J. Havighurst. *To Live on This Earth: American Indian Education.* Garden City, New York: Doubleday and Company, 1972. (23)

[50] Gallaher, Ruth A. "The Indian Agent in the United States before 1850." *Iowa Journal of History and Politics* 14 (January 1916): 3–55. (25)

[51] ——. "The Indian Agent in the United States since 1850." *Iowa Journal of History and Politics* 14 (April 1916): 173–238. (25)

[52] Garfield, Marvin H. "The Indian Question in Congress and in Kansas." *Kansas Historical Quarterly* 2 (February 1933): 29–44. (16)

[53] Gates, Paul W. "Indian Allotments Preceding the Dawes Act." In *The Frontier Challenge: Responses to the Trans-Mississippi West,* edited by John G. Clark,

pp. 141–170. Lawrence: University
Press of Kansas, 1971. (15)

[54] Gibson, Arrell M. *The Chickasaws.* Norman: University of Oklahoma Press,
1971. (26)

[55] Gittinger, Roy. *The Formation of the State
of Oklahoma (1803–1906).* Berkeley:
University of California Press, 1917.
New edition, Norman: University of
Oklahoma Press, 1939. (17)

*[56] Hagan, William T. *American Indians.*
Chicago: University of Chicago Press,
1961. (2)

[57] ———. *Indian Police and Judges: Experiments in Acculturation and Control.* New
Haven: Yale University Press, 1966. (17)

[58] ———. "Indian Policy after the Civil
War: The Reservation Experience." In
*American Indian Policy: Indiana Historical
Society Lectures 1970–1971,* pp. 20–36.
Indianapolis: Indiana Historical Society,
1971. (17)

[59] ———. "Private Property: The Indian's
Door to Civilization." *Ethnohistory* 3
(Spring 1956): 126–137. (15)

[60] ———. "The Reservation Policy: Too

Little and Too Late." In *Indian–White Relations: A Persistent Paradox,* edited by Jane F. Smith and Robert M. Kvasnicka, pp. 157–169. Washington, D.C.: Howard University Press, 1976. (17)

[61] _____. *The Sac and Fox Indians.* Norman: University of Oklahoma Press, 1958. (26)

[62] _____. *United States–Comanche Relations: The Reservation Years.* New Haven: Yale University Press, 1976. (26)

[63] Harmon, George Dewey. *Sixty Years of Indian Affairs, Political, Economic, and Diplomatic, 1789–1850.* Chapel Hill: University of North Carolina Press, 1941. (6)

[64] _____. "The United States Indian Policy in Texas, 1845–1860." *Mississippi Valley Historical Review* 17 (December 1930): 377–403. (11)

[65] Hertzberg, Hazel W. *The Search for an American Indian Identity: Modern Pan–Indian Movements.* Syracuse: Syracuse University Press, 1971. (18)

[66] Hood, Susan. "Termination of the Klamath Tribe in Oregon." *Ethnohistory* 19 (Fall 1972): 379–392. (22)

[67]   Hoopes, Alban W. *Indian Affairs and Their Administration, with Special Reference to the Far West, 1849–1860.* Philadelphia: University of Pennsylvania Press, 1932.   (11)

[68]   Horsman, Reginald. "American Indian Policy and the Origins of Manifest Destiny." *University of Birmingham Historical Journal* 11 (December 1968): 128–140.   (7)

[69]   _____. "American Indian Policy in the Old Northwest, 1783–1812." *William and Mary Quarterly* 18 (January 1961): 35–53.   (7)

[70]   _____. *Expansion and American Indian Policy, 1783–1812.* East Lansing: Michigan State University Press, 1967.   (7)

[71]   _____. *The Origin of Indian Removal, 1815–1824.* East Lansing: Michigan State University Press, 1970.   (9)

[72]   *Indian Education: A National Tragedy–A National Challenge.* Report of the Special Sub-Committee on Indian Education, Committee on Labor and Public Welfare, U. S. Senate. Washington, D.C.: Government Printing Office, 1969. Issued as *Senate Report* no. 501, 91st Congress, 1st session, serial 12836-1.   (24)

[73]   Jackson, Helen Hunt. *A Century of Dis-*

honor: A Sketch of the United States Government's Dealings with Some of the Indian Tribes. New York: Harper and Brothers, 1881.   (16)

[74]   Josephy, Alvin M., Jr. *The Nez Perce Indians and the Opening of the Northwest.* New Haven: Yale University Press, 1965.   (26)

*[75]   Josephy, Alvin M., Jr., ed. *Red Power: The American Indians' Fight for Freedom.* New York: American Heritage Press, 1971.   (22)

[76]   Kappler, Charles J., comp. *Indian Affairs: Laws and Treaties.* 5 volumes. Washington, D.C.: Government Printing Office, 1904–1941. Volume 2 has been reprinted as *Indian Treaties, 1778–1883.* New York: Interland Publishing, 1972.   (27)

[77]   Keller, Robert H., Jr. "The Protestant Churches and Grant's Peace Policy: A Study in Church–State Relations, 1869–1881." Ph.D. dissertation, University of Chicago, 1967.   (15)

[78]   Kelly, Lawrence C. "John Collier and the Indian New Deal: An Assessment." In *Indian–White Relations: A Persistent Paradox,* edited by Jane F. Smith and Robert M. Kvasnicka, pp. 227–241. Washing-

ton, D.C.: Howard University Press,
1976.   (20)

[79]   _____. *The Navajo Indians and Federal
Indian Policy, 1900–1935.* Tucson: University of Arizona Press, 1968.   (26)

[80]   Kelly, William H., ed. *Indian Affairs and
the Indian Reorganization Act: The Twenty
Year Record.* Tucson: University of Arizona, 1954.   (20)

[81]   Kelsey, Harry. "The Doolittle Report of
1867: Its Preparation and Short-
comings." *Arizona and the West* 17 (Summer 1975): 107–120.   (15)

[82]   _____. "William P. Dole and Mr. Lincoln's Indian Policy." *Journal of the West*
10 (July 1971): 484–492.   (13)

[83]   Kickingbird, Kirke, and Karen Ducheneaux. *One Hundred Million Acres.* New
York: Macmillan Company, 1973.   (22)

[84]   Koch, Lena Clara. "The Federal Indian
Policy in Texas, 1845–1860." *Southwest-
ern Historical Quarterly* 28 (January 1925):
223–234; (April 1925): 259–286; 29
(July 1925): 19–35; (October 1925):
98–127.   (11)

[85]   La Farge, Oliver. "Termination of Federal Supervision: Disintegration and the

American Indian." *Annals of the American Academy of Political and Social Science* 311 (May 1957): 41–46. (22)

[86] LeDuc, Thomas. "The Work of the Indian Claims Commission under the Act of 1946." *Pacific Historical Review* 26 (February 1957): 1–16. (21)

[87] Lee, R. Alton. "Indian Citizenship and the Fourteenth Amendment." *South Dakota History* 4 (Spring 1974): 198–221. (16)

[88] Leupp, Francis E. *The Indian and His Problem*. New York: Charles Scribner's Sons, 1910. (18)

[89] Loos, John L. "William Clark, Indian Agent." *Kansas Quarterly* 3 (Fall 1971): 29–38. (25)

[90] Lurie, Nancy Oestreich. "The Indian Claims Commission Act." *Annals of the American Academy of Political and Social Science* 311 (May 1957): 56–70. (21)

[91] ———. "Menominee Termination: From Reservation to Colony." *Human Organization* 31 (Fall 1972): 257–270. (22)

[92] McCluggage, Robert W. "The Senate and Indian Land Titles, 1800–1825." *Western Historical Quarterly* 1 (October 1970): 415–425. (7)

*[93]   McNickle, D'Arcy. *Native American Trib-alism: Indian Survivals and Renewals.* New York: Oxford University Press, 1973.   (2, 20)

*[94]   ———. *They Came Here First: The Epic of the American Indian.* Philadelphia: J. B. Lippincott Company, 1949.   (2)

[95]   McReynolds, Edwin C. *The Seminoles.* Norman: University of Oklahoma Press, 1957.   (26)

[96]   Madigan, La Verne. *The American Indian Relocation Program.* New York: Association on American Indian Affairs, 1956.   (21)

[97]   Malin, James C. *Indian Policy and Westward Expansion.* Bulletin of the University of Kansas Humanistic Studies, volume 2, no. 3. Lawrence: University of Kansas, 1921.   (11)

[98]   Mardock, Robert Winston. *The Reformers and the American Indian.* Columbia: University of Missouri Press, 1971.   (14)

[99]   Mekeel, Scudder. "An Appraisal of the Indian Reorganization Act." *American Anthropologist* 46 (April–June 1944): 209–217.   (20)

[100]   Meriam, Lewis, and others. *The Problem of Indian Administration.* Institute for Government Research, Studies in Ad-

ministration. Baltimore: Johns Hopkins
Press, 1928. (19)

[101] Meyer, Roy W. *History of the Santee Sioux:
United States Indian Policy on Trial.* Lincoln: University of Nebraska Press,
1967. (26)

[102] Miles, Edwin A. "After John Marshall's
Decision: *Worcester* v. *Georgia* and the
Nullification Crisis." *Journal of Southern
History* 39 (November 1973): 519–544. (10)

[103] Miles, William. " 'Enamoured with
Colonization': Isaac McCoy's Plan of Indian Reform." *Kansas Historical Quarterly*
38 (Autumn 1972): 268–286. (9)

[104] Mohr, Walter H. *Federal Indian Relations, 1774–1788.* Philadelphia: University of Pennsylvania Press, 1933. (6)

[105] Morgan, Dale L. "The Administration of
Indian Affairs in Utah, 1851–1858." *Pacific Historical Review* 17 (November
1948): 383–409. (12)

[106] Morton, Ohland. "Confederate Government Relations with the Five Civilized Tribes." *Chronicles of Oklahoma* 31
(Summer 1953): 189–204; (Autumn
1953): 299–322. (13)

[107] Neils, Elaine M. *Reservation to City: In-*

dian Migration and Federal Relocation.
Chicago: University of Chicago, Department of Geography, 1971.   (21)

[108] Nevins, Allan. "Helen Hunt Jackson,
       Sentimentalist vs. Realist." *American
       Scholar* 10 (Summer 1941): 269–285.   (16)

[109] Odell, Ruth. *Helen Hunt Jackson (H. H.).*
       New York: D. Appleton–Century Com-
       pany, 1939.   (16)

[110] Olson, James C. *Red Cloud and the Sioux
       Problem.* Lincoln: University of Nebraska
       Press, 1965.   (26)

[111] Otis, D. S. *The Dawes Act and the Allotment
       of Indian Lands.* Edited by Francis Paul
       Prucha. Norman: University of Okla-
       homa Press, 1973.   (16)

[112] Parman, Donald L. *The Navajos and the
       New Deal.* New Haven: Yale University
       Press, 1976.   (20)

[113] Peake, Ora Brooks. *A History of the
       United States Indian Factory System,
       1795–1822.* Denver: Sage Books, 1954.   (7)

[114] Philp, Kenneth R. "Albert B. Fall and the
       Protest from the Pueblos, 1921–23." *Ari-
       zona and the West* 12 (Autumn 1970):
       237–254.   (19)

[115] ———. "Herbert Hoover's New Era: A False Dawn for the American Indian, 1929–1932." *Rocky Mountain Social Science Journal* 9 (April 1972): 53–60.　　(19)

[116] ———. "John Collier and the American Indian, 1920–1945." In *Essays on Radicalism in Contemporary America,* edited by Leon Borden Blair, pp. 63–80. Austin: University of Texas Press, 1972.　　(19)

[117] ———. "John Collier and the Controversy over the Wheeler–Howard Bill." In *Indian–White Relations: A Persistent Paradox,* edited by Jane F. Smith and Robert M. Kvasnicka, pp. 171–200. Washington, D.C.: Howard University Press, 1976.　　(20)

[118] ———. "John Collier and the Crusade to Protect Indian Religious Freedom, 1920–1926." *Journal of Ethnic Studies* 1 (Spring 1973): 22–38.　　(19)

[119] ———. *John Collier's Crusade for Indian Reform, 1920–1954.* Tucson: University of Arizona Press, 1976.　　(19)

[120]   Pound, Merritt B. *Benjamin Hawkins—
        Indian Agent.* Athens: University of
        Georgia Press, 1951.   (25)

[121]   Price, Monroe E. *Law and the American
        Indian: Readings, Notes and Cases.* In-
        dianapolis: Bobbs-Merrill Company,
        1973.   (24)

[122]   Priest, Loring Benson. *Uncle Sam's Step-
        children: The Reformation of United States
        Indian Policy, 1865–1887.* New Bruns-
        wick: Rutgers University Press, 1942.   (14)

[123]   Prucha, Francis Paul. *American Indian
        Policy in Crisis: Christian Reformers and the
        Indian, 1865–1900.* Norman: University
        of Oklahoma Press, 1976.   (14)

[124]   ———. "American Indian Policy in the
        1840s: Visions of Reform." In *The Fron-
        tier Challenge: Responses to the Trans-
        Mississippi West,* edited by John G. Clark,
        pp. 81–110. Lawrence: University Press
        of Kansas, 1971.   (10)

[125]   ———. *American Indian Policy in the
        Formative Years: The Indian Trade and In-
        tercourse Acts, 1790–1834.* Cambridge:
        Harvard University Press, 1962.   (6)

[126]   ———. "Andrew Jackson's Indian
        Policy: A Reassessment." *Journal of Amer-*

ican History 56 (December 1969): 527–539.   (9)

[127]   ———. *A Bibliographical Guide to the History of Indian –White Relations in the United States.* Chicago: University of Chicago Press, 1977.   (2)

[128]   ———. *Lewis Cass and American Indian Policy.* Detroit: Wayne State University Press, 1967.   (25)

[129]   ———. *The Sword of the Republic: The United States Army on the Frontier, 1783 – 1846.* New York: Macmillan Company, 1969.   (25)

[130]   Prucha, Francis Paul, ed. *Americanizing the American Indians: Writings by the "Friends of the Indian" 1880 –1900.* Cambridge: Harvard University Press, 1973.   (16)

[131]   ———. *Documents of United States Indian Policy.* Lincoln: University of Nebraska Press, 1975.   (27)

[132]   Rahill, Peter James. *The Catholic Indian Missions and Grant's Peace Policy, 1870 – 1884.* Washington, D.C.: Catholic University of America Press, 1953.   (15)

[133]   Reeve, Frank D. "The Federal Indian Policy in New Mexico, 1858–1880." *New Mexico Historical Review* 12 (July 1937):

218–269; 13 (January 1938): 14–62; (April 1938): 146–191; (July 1938): 261–313.   (17)

[134] Rogin, Michael Paul. *Fathers and Children: Andrew Jackson and the Subjugation of the American Indian.* New York: Alfred A. Knopf, 1975.   (9)

[135] Royce, Charles C., comp. *Indian Land Cessions in the United States.* Eighteenth Annual Report of the Bureau of American Ethnology, 1896–1897, part 2. Washington, D.C.: Government Printing Office, 1899. Reprinted, New York: Arno Press, 1971.   (27)

[136] Satz, Ronald N. *American Indian Policy in the Jacksonian Era.* Lincoln: University of Nebraska Press, 1975.   (10)

[137] Schmeckebier, Laurence, F. *The Office of Indian Affairs: Its History, Activities, and Organization.* Institute for Government Research, Service Monographs of the United States Government, no. 48. Baltimore: Johns Hopkins Press, 1927.   (25)

[138] Seymour, Flora Warren. *Indian Agents of the Old Frontier.* New York: D. Appleton-Century Company, 1941.   (25)

[139] Sheehan, Bernard W. *Seeds of Extinction:*

Jeffersonian Philanthropy and the American Indian. Chapel Hill: University of North Carolina Press, 1973. (7)

[140] Smith, Michael T. "The History of Indian Citizenship." *Great Plains Journal* 10 (Fall 1970): 25–35. (16)

[141] ———. "The Wheeler–Howard Act of 1934: The Indian New Deal." *Journal of the West* 10 (July 1971): 521–534. (20)

[142] Sorkin, Alan L. *American Indians and Federal Aid.* Washington, D.C.: Brookings Institution, 1971. (23)

*[143] Spicer, Edward H. *A Short History of the Indians of the United States.* New York: Van Nostrand-Reinhold Company, 1969. (3)

[144] Stein, Gary C. "The Indian Citizenship Act of 1924." *New Mexico Historical Review* 47 (July 1972): 257–274. (16)

[145] Sterling, Everett W. "The Indian Reservation System on the North Central Plains." *Montana, the Magazine of Western History* 14 (April 1964): 92–100. (17)

[146] Szasz, Margaret G. *Education and the American Indian: The Road to Self-Determination, 1928–1973.* Albuquerque: University of New Mexico Press, 1974. (23)

[147] ———. "Indian Reform in a Decade of Prosperity." *Montana, the Magazine of Western History* 20 (Winter 1970): 16–27.   (19)

[148] Taylor, Graham D. "Anthropologists, Reformers, and the Indian New Deal." *Prologue: The Journal of the National Archives* 7 (Fall 1975): 151–162.   (20)

[149] ———. "The Tribal Alternative to Bureaucracy: The Indian's New Deal, 1933–1945." *Journal of the West* 13 (January 1974): 128–142.   (20)

[150] Trennert, Robert A., Jr. *Alternative to Extinction: Federal Indian Policy and the Beginnings of the Reservation System, 1846–51.* Philadelphia: Temple University Press, 1975.   (12)

[151] Tyler, S. Lyman. *A History of Indian Policy.* Washington, D.C.: Department of the Interior, Bureau of Indian Affairs, 1973.   (3, 20)

[152] ———. "The Recent Urbanization of the American Indian." In *Essays on the American West, 1973–1974,* edited by Thomas G. Alexander, pp. 43–62. Provo, Utah: Brigham Young University Press, 1975.   (21)

[153] Unrau, William E. "The Civilian as Indian Agent: Villain or Victim?" *Western*

Historical Quarterly 3 (October 1972):
405–420. (25)

[154] Utley, Robert M. "The Celebrated Peace
Policy of General Grant." *North Dakota
History* 20 (July 1953): 121–142. (15)

[155] _____. *Frontier Regulars: The United
States Army and the Indian, 1866–1891.*
New York: Macmillan Company, 1973. (25)

[156] _____. *Frontiersmen in Blue: The United
States Army and the Indian, 1848–1865.*
New York: Macmillan Company, 1967. (25)

[157] _____. *The Last Days of the Sioux Nation.*
New Haven: Yale University Press, 1963. (26)

[158] Vance, John T. "The Congressional
Mandate and the Indian Claims Com-
mission." *North Dakota Law Review* 45
(Spring 1969): 325–336. (21)

*[159] Van Every, Dale. *Disinherited: The Lost
Birthright of the American Indian.* New
York: Morrow, 1966. (9)

[160] Viola, Herman J. *Thomas L. McKenney:
Architect of America's Early Indian Policy,
1816–1830.* Chicago: Swallow Press,
1974. (8)

[161] Waddell, Jack O., and O. Michael Watson, eds. *The American Indian in Urban*

Society. Boston: Little Brown and Company, 1971.   (21)

[162]   Waltmann, Henry G. "Circumstantial Reformer: President Grant and the Indian Problem." *Arizona and the West* 13 (Winter 1971): 323–342.   (15)

[163]   Wardell, Morris L. *A Political History of the Cherokee Nation, 1838–1907.* Norman: University of Oklahoma Press, 1938.   (26)

[164]   Washburn, Wilcomb E. *The Assault on Indian Tribalism: The General Allotment Law (Dawes Act) of 1887.* Philadelphia: J. B. Lippincott Company, 1975.   (15)

*[165]   _____. *The Indian in America.* New York: Harper and Row, 1975.   (3, 20)

[166]   _____. *Red Man's Land / White Man's Law: A Study of the Past and Present Status of the American Indian.* New York: Charles Scribner's Sons, 1971.   (24)

[167]   Washburn, Wilcomb E., ed. *The American Indian and the United States: A Documentary History.* 4 volumes. New York: Random House, 1973.   (27)

[168]   Watkins, Arthur V. "Termination of Federal Supervision: The Removal of

Restrictions over Indian Property and Person." *Annals of the American Academy of Political and Social Science* 311 (May 1957): 47–55. (22)

[169] Way, Royal B. "The United States Factory System for Trading with the Indians, 1796–1822." *Mississippi Valley Historical Review* 6 (September 1919): 220–235. (8)

[170] Wesley, Edgar B. "The Government Factory System among the Indians, 1795–1822." *Journal of Economic and Business History* 4 (May 1932): 487–511. (8)

[171] Whitner, Robert L. "The Methodist Episcopal Church and Grant's Peace Policy: A Study of the Methodist Agencies, 1870–1882." Ph.D. dissertation, University of Minnesota, 1959. (15)

[172] Wilkins, Thurman. *Cherokee Tragedy: The Story of the Ridge Family and the Decimation of a People.* New York: Macmillan Company, 1970. (10)

[173] Wissler, Clark. *Indian Cavalcade; or, Life on the Old-Time Indian Reservations.* New York: Sheridan House, 1938. Reissued as *Red Man Reservations.* New York: Macmillan Company, 1971. (17)

[174]   Young, Mary E. "Indian Removal and Land Allotment: The Civilized Tribes and Jacksonian Justice." *American Historical Review* 64 (October 1958): 31–45.   (9)

[175]   ———. *Redskins, Ruffleshirts, and Rednecks: Indian Allotments in Alabama and Mississippi, 1830–1860.* Norman: University of Oklahoma Press, 1961.   (9)